Law of Attr-Action for Entrepreneurs

Advanced Identity Shifting Secrets to Manifest the Income & Impact You Deserve

Law of Attraction Short Reads, Book 4

**Written by Elena G.Rivers
Copyright © Elena G.Rivers 2020**

Copyright Notice

All rights reserved. No part of this publication may be reproduced, stored in a retrieval system, or transmitted, in any form or by any means, electronic, mechanical, photocopying, recording or otherwise, without the prior written permission of the author and the publishers.

The scanning, uploading, and distribution of this book via the Internet or via any other means without the permission of the author is illegal and punishable by law.

Please purchase only authorized electronic editions, and do not participate in or encourage electronic piracy of copyrighted materials.

Disclaimer Notice

Please note the information contained in this document is for inspirational and entertainment purposes only.

Every attempt has been made to provide accurate, up to date, and completely reliable information. No warranties of any kind are expressed or implied.

Readers acknowledge that the author is not engaging in the rendering of legal, financial, health, medical, or professional advice.

By reading this publication, the reader agrees that under no circumstances are we responsible for any losses, direct or indirect, which are incurred as a result of the use of the information contained within this document, including, but not limited to, errors, omissions, or inaccuracies.

Contents

Intro – Why Traditional Law of Attraction Techniques Aren't Enough for Entrepreneurs 6

Transform Your Mindset to Grow Your Income and Impact 12

The Hidden Dangers of Manifesting from Your Old Identity 19

Why "Normalization" Is the #1 Step to Start Shifting Your Identity and Reality 22

The Art of Mindful Action & Natural Productivity 24

Unleash Unstoppable Motivation (no more overthinking) 27

Why Full Responsibility Is Sexy and Attractive (and the Universe Will LOVE You for It!) 29

Mindful Clarity for Magnetic Confidence (don't let your old self block you!) 32

Mindful Clarity Exercise (know your *why* and your biz model like your life depends on it) 33

How Curiosity-Based Mindset and Mindful Discipline Can Help You Manifest Faster (without stress or burnouts) 38

Releasing the Perfectionist Syndrome 42

Use Your "Who" to Get Out of Your Head 50

Whatever Happens, It Happens FOR You! 52

How NOT to Learn (Avoid This Trap) 59

The Real Secret Behind Mindful Learning (hidden dangers of social media) 63

Success is a Relaxed State (Stop Contracting and Start Expanding)..66
The Honest Truth about the Mirror Principle in Business (use it to your advantage) 71
Why Coming Up with Your Perfect Client Avatar is NOT Enough Until You Do This One Thing! ..79
Use Energetic Micro Niche Marketing to Manifest Your Dream Customers with Ease 82
The Total Immersion Formula to Eliminate Limiting Beliefs on Autopilot 84
Create Awesome Process-Based Goals (No More Anxiety!)..90
Total Freedom from "What Will Other People Think of Me?" 92
Why Strategy Isn't Enough (the Invisible Force of Self-Image)..96
The ONE Exercise You Must NEVER STOP Doing!..98
Shift Yourself Out of Overwhelm (works like magic!) 103
Be a LOA-Preneur, You Can Do This! 105
Expert Resources and Biz Ideas for LOA Entrepreneurs... 106

Intro – Why Traditional Law of Attraction Techniques Aren't Enough for Entrepreneurs

It's time to focus on thoughts, actions, and decisions that fully align with your vision so that you can create a life of freedom, fulfillment, and abundance!

So how can you transform your business, life, and income with the Law of Attraction? And what exactly is *the Law of Attraction for Entrepreneurs*?

To keep it simple, the Law of Attr-action for Entrepreneurs is a unique system based on mindful action, understanding your higher Self, the universal laws of abundance and gratitude, as well as practical, honest, and authentic loved-based marketing strategies.

However, the core principles behind the methodology I share in this book are rooted in deep mindset and energy work that helps you shift your personality on a core level and manifest your entrepreneurial dreams faster.

Let me start with what this book isn't and who shouldn't read it. I realize that not everyone is ready to manifest an abundance through their own business. If that's you, I don't want to waste your time and energy that might be better put elsewhere.

This isn't a basic Law of Attraction book. So, it won't tell you just to think positively, create a vision board, and keep affirming what you want. Don't get me wrong, nothing against affirmations and vision boards! All LOA techniques such as scripting, visualizing, affirming, and whatnot work very well; however, they're not effective if a person is unwilling to change his or her mindset and energy. A person with a poor mindset might spend the whole day affirming, "I'm so rich," but still feel unworthy of success, therefore sending a vibration of lack to the Universe.

All LOA methods you've likely encountered are tactics, but to be effective, they need to form part of a bigger strategy. And the best strategy to attract what you want is to become a vibrational match to it. If you want to manifest through your own business, then all your products, services and marketing messages must vibrate at a particular level to help you manifest the abundance and impact you desire. The best way to do so is by changing your identity so that your thoughts, feelings, and actions align with what you want.

Needless to say, that action is required to succeed with this book; this is why the title is what it is – *the Law of Attr-action*.

I don't mean to sound condescending, but I don't have the energy to deal with people who expect something for nothing.

All successful heart-led leaders and entrepreneurs take action. Even the manifestation gurus who tell you no action is required, keep taking action every day to grow their business and impact, it's just who they are. They can't stop!

Oh, and it's not a book teaching you how to win the lottery fast. It's not for people who want something to be given to them without even trying to add any value to the world.

However, if your problem is that you have a dream of starting a business, but have no idea what that could be, then this book will help you gain clarity. You're on the right path. As long as you want to add value and create a business that helps people, you're good to go, and all your answers will be unfolding as you keep taking actions suggested in this book.

But this book isn't only for new entrepreneurs or those who are just starting out. If you're a seasoned entrepreneur, but perhaps you feel like you hit the invisible ceiling, or maybe your passion and purpose fade away and you're feeling stuck, then this book will give you valuable tools you can use to shift to the next level.

I know what it's like to feel stuck in business. You work hard, you apply new marketing strategies, yet nothing seems to work. If that's your case, and you already tried all the external solutions, worked with marketing experts and whatnot, and now suspect the issue is internal, then this book will help you. There's nothing wrong with you; you just need to learn to work with the universal laws and make a few simple fixes in your mindset and energy.

Also, this isn't a business book. I'm not a business consultant or strategist. This book won't teach you how to set up a business, or the legalities of it; for that you'd need to talk to a professional accountant or attorney. And I can't give you the hottest marketing tactic for this year or the best business opportunity. I have no business opportunity to sell you in this book. The best opportunity will always be the one that aligns with your strengths and passions, and this book is designed to give you some clarity on your path.

As a bonus, at the end of this book, I share some ideas you can grab and use to start and grow your business, whether you want to do something on the side, or be a full-time entrepreneur. But just like with manifestation tools or methods, there's no such thing as the best way to start a business because that depends on many factors, such as your skills, background, country, socioeconomic status, and, most importantly, your mindset and energy.

And this is what this book focuses on. It bridges the gap between the world of business and the law of attraction.

It focuses on the mindset and energy shifts you need to become the person who can manifest a business of your dreams.

This book will help you:
-Determine the blocks that are preventing you from starting or growing your business
-Cultivate your confidence muscle while unleashing your authenticity
-Get super clear on your vision so that you can focus on growing a business of freedom
-Eliminate self-doubt, perfectionism, limiting beliefs, and fear of failure
-Prevent burnouts and low energy
-Feel fulfilled and receive appreciation
-Attract the right customers to your business so that you enjoy what you do
-Discover how to overcome money blocks
-Understand how to transform anxiety into excitement and empowerment

This book is perfect for:
-professionals who would love to quit their corporate job, or launch a passion business on the side, yet have no idea where to start
-inspiring entrepreneurs who tried different business opportunities and nothing seemed to work, even though they completed all the business programs
-empaths and healers who want to share their message with the world but feel stuck
-creatives, writers, artists, and authors who would love to turn their work into consistent income while creating a legacy
-coaches, consultants, and service providers who are fed up with not attracting the right clients to their business and seek to grow by attracting quality people who are willing to pay higher prices
-established business owners who feel stuck at a certain income level, even though they work hard and have a good strategy, nothing seems to work anymore

In other words, it's time to do some mindset and energy makeover and release what's no longer serving you!

Real success and happiness start with self-awareness. If you want to create a meaningful business and life, you cannot switch off your feelings and emotions. You need to dive deep and realize what's going on. Make decisions in alignment with what you want so that you design a business you love.

You don't have to achieve to make other people happy. To be free, you need to understand what you want and start creating based on that.

If you follow the strategies I'll teach you in this book; you'll be able to achieve your goals faster and with less stress.

Everyone has something they can turn into a business; it's just a matter of diving deep, finding that thing, and overcoming mental battles.

Transform Your Mindset to Grow Your Income and Impact

Success leaves clues, and you can learn a lot from studying successful entrepreneurs. However, the number one mistake that most new entrepreneurs make is that they don't really know how to study success. They don't know what kind of questions to ask. When looking at someone who's achieved financial freedom, the question they ask is usually: *so what did you do? What's your business model?*

While this isn't a wrong question, a better question should be: *how do you think?*

There are zillions of business models, and all of them can work. What really matters is knowing yourself good enough to determine your right path, so that you can start and grow a business that aligns with your strengths, passions, talents, values, and visions.

Yes, successful entrepreneurs also understand the importance of good strategy and business models. However, a person could have the best business strategist as his or her mentor yet still fail if one doesn't think like a successful person.

It's all about transforming your mindset so that you can change the way you do things. The good news is that you can reverse-engineer the most effective success patterns and use them to change your reality.

Successful entrepreneurs and leaders, people like Bob Proctor, Oprah, or Tony Robbins, do things in a certain way and think in a certain way. Let's suppose that an experienced coach and entrepreneur such as Tony Robbins gives away his business to someone who's just starting out. He shares the manual with the strategy and what-not. Do you think that a beginner would be successful? Do you believe they could handle so much responsibility at once? Probably not, because their identity is still not aligned with such a big mission. To run a big coaching company, you need a mindset of a person who feels it's normal for them to run the show on a bigger scale.

Now, this is just one example in one specific industry (coaching). I used this example as I assume most readers are familiar with Tony Robbins, Bob Proctor, and Oprah Winfrey. But this comparison applies to every venture, project, or business idea.

You need to start with a vision that excites you- whether it's a blueprint for a new business or the next level of success in the existing one.

After you have designed the vision of that business, you need to see yourself as the new, more empowered version of yourself, or the 2.0 version of yourself.

What's this person like? What are his or her habits, thoughts, and feelings?

This is a very empowering question, and it should give you a clear indication of what you need to improve.

For example, in my case, I used to struggle with schedules, seriously! I tried everything, including pushing myself into a 5 AM club, which wasn't for me. But, once I took some time to focus on my vision, and I saw my new, upgraded self, I immediately understood what I needed to do.

Instead of trying hard to wake up early while still defining myself as someone who is an artist and hates sticking to schedules, I described myself as someone who loves writing in the mornings and who adores mindful discipline. I began shifting my identity. Before I knew it, I could naturally get up early and work on my books early in the morning, before breakfast!

Change can be very hard. And it can get even more frustrating for someone who did lots of personal development, tried applying different "self-improvement" techniques, yet still ended up in the same negative loop.

I was there too, and it was very frustrating. I felt I wasn't good enough, and I always had to push myself and improve myself. This is where mainstream self-development or self-improvement can go wrong.

What happens is that you try hard to change things and encounter more and more resistance; what you resist persists! Then you end up feeling upset or even guilty that nothing worked and that others could do it, but you couldn't (more on comparing yourself to others later).

After realizing that mainstream self-help wasn't really for me, I went on a quest to find my answers. I wanted to know how to create a permanent change or a profound identity shift that results in a reality shift.

I travelled the world, met different people, and learned from various mentors. My curiosity led me to study them and the success patterns they followed. And one thing they all had in common is that they knew how to change their identity so that they could become what they wanted to attract.

In other words, I realized that you don't always attract what you want (yes miracles happen, but this is beyond the scope of this book). Instead, **you attract who you are.**

As Doctor Joe Dispenza says: "Your personality creates your personal reality."

Most people get it the other way round: *Just put me in a better place, give me this business opportunity where it's all done for me! Make money for me, and then I'll change!*

As I'm sure you can guess, such thinking leads to nowhere, or it can lead to temporary success that makes you sad, exhausted, or disappointed.

The most powerful thing you can do for yourself is to change your identity and become a new person. Erase bad experiences and consciously focus your mind on good ones. Swap complaints with gratitude. Be a high-value person who attracts high-value people.

See yourself as the entrepreneur you want to be. But don't chase it and don't get too stuck in wanting and desiring. Be that person now by embodying their actions, habits, feelings, and thoughts.

Many people get it wrong. They start thinking of themselves as 6 or 7 figure entrepreneurs, but rather than of exploring the mindsets of their new selves, they merely focus on superficial items like clothes or cars.

Don't get me wrong; there's nothing wrong with treating yourself to something nice and looking good. If you want to buy yourself something nice because you genuinely love the item and you can afford it, and it makes you feel good, then why not?

But, if a person tries hard to buy something he or she can't afford just to look wealthy or impress others, this is where resistance will start appearing again.

What you want to do instead is to:

1.Design the vision of your ideal business.

2.Focus on *the Future You* from the inside; what are your habits, routines, mindsets?

I'd even go as far as asking yourself: *what new problems do you have, and what makes you feel angry?*

You see, the new, 2.0 version of yourself doesn't have your current issues, but it may have unique better quality problems.

For example, a new entrepreneur's problem could be: *how can I work on my business and grow it while still doing a full-time job?*

How can I get my first client, or how can I reach a full-time income with my business?

But, the new, 2.0 version of yourself, who is, let's say a 7 figure entrepreneur, may be experiencing a different quality of problems such as:

-*What's the best tax structure for my business? How can I find a high-level accountant?*

-*How do I attract highly motivated people to my team, and how do I lead them?*

Analyze your current thoughts, beliefs, and habits and compare them to those of your new, 2.0 version of yourself.

Then, focus on one simple change at a time by literally walking into that new, more empowered version of yourself.

Allow yourself to transform on a deeper level and make your subconscious mind believe that change is safe. After all, you're already that new 2.0 version, and you're taking action from a place of confidence. It's normal for you to take action and love it; it's natural for you to grow your business and attract amazing clients.

Imagine your dream life and business. Envision your impact and income. Who's the person who's already making it happen? Who's that new, more empowered 2.0 version?

Be that person already! Each mindset shift taken in the right direction helps re-program your subconscious mind and make it believe that change isn't only safe but also possible.

The Hidden Dangers of Manifesting from Your Old Identity

The main danger of manifesting from your old identity is that you'll need a lot of willpower and can eventually end up burned out, as I did.

You see, in my "previous life," I had no idea about this identity shifting stuff. So, I worked very hard to prove myself in front of others, and I manifested a successful business. The process was lots of blood, sweat, and tears. But my problem was that I was still my old identity, I was still very insecure, and I didn't feel worthy of abundance. Yes, I had a bit more money and success. But, I lost my zest for life. I ended up very sick and depressed.

And this happens to many entrepreneurs who try to manifest from their old paradigms or as their old selves. They think that once they manifest an incredible business, they'll change. But it hardly ever works that way.

So, there I was- even though I manifested a profitable business, I felt empty inside, and every day was a struggle. Even though I could travel the world, which I did, I still felt empty and couldn't mindfully enjoy my travels.

I asked myself: *is that it*? I thought that after achieving all this success, I'd feel differently. And then, something inside me told me: *first manifest your new self, authenticity, and happiness, and the rest will follow*.

I liked that idea, but my old self prevailed once again, So, I hustled hard to try to get to the next level. I thought that maybe if I set a bigger money goal, I'd get my passion and fulfillment back.

I hired a mentor, who was a very successful entrepreneur with a rigorous schedule; he worked himself to the ground pretty much every day. He was a well-respected marketer and productivity expert who charged a lot for his services.

For a while, I got attracted to this rather masculine energy thinking that *maybe it's what I needed, perhaps I just need to work harder, reach the next level, and then I could experience that fleeting feeling of achievement once again.*

Maybe...I could be the female version of that mentor? Once again, it was the old ego and old identity speaking through me. *Yea that makes sense; I could be like him and charge super high prices; people would obey me, I'd have the power to influence them.*

And that mentor and all his team kept telling me- *just keep pushing outside your comfort zone! Then you'll feel like a new person again.*

As you can probably guess, it didn't end very well, and I only ended up with more anxiety and burnout, and then my business revenue began shrinking every day.

The hustle, grind, new strategy, new mentor...nothing worked, because even though I was upgrading my sales funnels, I didn't upgrade myself.

Now I'm grateful for this experience, and I'm a new person; I learned a lot about myself and the world. Eventually, I quit my old business and decided to focus on what I loved doing the most – writing!

I dedicated lots of time to doing inner work to shift my identity, which is exactly what I want to teach you through this book. After all, you want to create a business you love; you want to attract people you can help. Why push if you can pull?

So many entrepreneurs manifest from their old identity, and very often from old doubts and fears. Yes, they can create a successful business, but if deep inside, they're full of doubts, their reality will sooner or later start reflecting that.

What you want to focus on instead is the act of making things feel normal for you.

Why "Normalization" Is the #1 Step to Start Shifting Your Identity and Reality

It's normal for you to read this book. You got it on Kindle, another eBook platform, or perhaps in print or audio. There's probably one format you prefer, and using it is normal for you.

You don't need to overthink it. You don't need to try and feel worthy of reading books or eBooks. You're a person who prefers to read eBooks instead of regular books, or the other way round. Or perhaps you're a person who really enjoys listening to inspirational audiobooks in your car.

It's normal for you; it's just who you are.

Such an act of normalization can also be applied to your vision for business and life.

Imagine you're a 6 or 7 figure business owner right now. Or whatever goal you have. Perhaps, right now, you just want to build a side income from your passion; that's fine too, whatever it is you desire. See yourself as if it was happening right here and right now.

What are your thoughts and reactions to things? Make a conscious decision to apply them to your current reality, and watch it transform. It's as simple as that! Now this was only the beginning or the aperitif. We'll be diving into the main courses of this amazing reality creation in the next chapters!

Oh, and don't forget to read this book as the new, 2.0 version of yourself. Why not?

You already are that person; that new version of you already exists! It's just a matter of aligning yourself with it through your thoughts, actions, habits, and feelings.

Let's do this!

The Art of Mindful Action & Natural Productivity

To launch the new version of yourself, you'll need to take aligned action and be consistent. Just like with anything in life, the action is needed to make your vision manifest into physical reality.

But, here's where many readers ask me: *how do I start taking action as my new self, all from a new paradigm? What if I do something that is not aligned with my new vision?*

And, more often than not, by getting lost in so many questions, they eventually find excuses. *Maybe I should wait with this identity shifting stuff? Or perhaps I can try something else?*

As a result, they get stuck in procrastination and inaction. Here's how to overcome it with what I like to call "mindful action and natural productivity."

First of all, we don't procrastinate because of a lack of routine. Even with the best routine or schedule, you can still procrastinate. So many people get stuck looking for the perfect morning ritual, whereas in reality, the best one is the one that you enjoy and makes you feel excited to get up.

But it's not only about your morning ritual, but the *whole day ritual*! A person could do a fantastic morning ritual and then sit and complain all day. Or they could start the day well and then procrastinate again and never complete the most critical activities to start or grow their business.

Planning and creating routines work only when you understand the fundamentals; and in this case, you need to motivate yourself, you need something that makes you tick. I could write another book on morning rituals and success routines for entrepreneurs, but once again, what's more important is that you develop a deep motivation muscle.

Most people get motivated by escaping from pain. For example, *I'll do the sales calls, because I have bills to pay and I don't want to get evicted.*

Or: *I will work hard to prove others wrong so that they don't laugh at me and don't tell me I'm a failure.*

Don't get me wrong; using pain for motivation can be very effective, and yes, this is how most people and most entrepreneurs operate. Chances are that your old self also operated from such a reality.

Also, many people procrastinate because they focus too much on the negatives; they're too afraid to take action because they are worried it might not work. In other words, they feed their procrastination muscle and must rely on pain-based motivation or extreme will power to get something done.

Ask yourself, is this how the new version of you wants to operate?

Pain motivation is all about taking action for survival. While I don't fully discredit it, I used it when I was at the lowest point in my life and I had to rebuild myself as fast as I could. Back then, my motivation was to be able to pay the bills and survive. It worked back then, and I'm grateful. But once I manifested my income goal, I also hit the invisible ceiling and got comfortable. This is where many entrepreneurs end up. Luckily, there's a better way! You can raise your standards and think and act as a new, 2.0 version of yourself and operate from love for creating and building, not the pain of escaping. This can be such a powerful shift, and this is how all successful leaders and entrepreneurs operate.

Also, pain-induced motivation implies you're not successful now and are in a rat race of escaping from what you don't like. This is how you activate the LOA in a negative way. Your focus is on what you don't want. You don't want to work in a job you hate, and you don't want to serve clients you don't like, etc.

Your reality will eventually start reflecting such an attitude, so even if you begin manifesting more money, you'll still be escaping without ever being able to enjoy what you've created. You know my story, I've been there too.

Instead, see yourself as a powerful creator and take mindful action from a place of love and gratitude. Use the pleasure-based motivation where there's no more ceiling and no more pain. Focus on the revolutionary heights you can achieve.

Focus on people you want to work with and attract to your business, don't take action to merely avoid attracting clients you don't want to serve- as it'll automatically switch your attention to what you don't want.

And the Law of Attraction says- what you focus on expands! What you constantly think about, you get!

Unleash Unstoppable Motivation (no more overthinking!)

When you are in a pleasure-based motivation, you thrive, and you also fall in love with what you do. To give you an example, there are specific tasks in my business that I didn't enjoy doing, one of them being accounting.

I used to hate accounting and would always avoid it until I had to do it to file my taxes. But after switching to love-based motivation, I began to enjoy working with numbers. Now, it's a monthly ritual I look forward to. I play my favorite music, I organize my invoices and share them with my accountant.

Now, everything is done on time, and my accountant can do a better job to help me. And what's more important, I know exactly where my money goes; and as they say, "what gets measured gets managed."

To manifest a business goal I'm working on now, I had to change my identity to someone who likes numbers. I could no longer hide like a little kid who says,: *Oh, but I don't like math, I prefer to write instead.*

Such a simple mindset shift that gave me so much peace of mind!

When I was in a pain-based motivation, I'd always wait for that dreaded deadline: *if I don't do this, I might get audited. What if I get a fine because I'm late with my taxes?*

Oh, and did I mention that back then, I would always attract accountants who would also wait and procrastinate? Then, of course, I'd complain to other business owners with similar pain and fear-based mindset. *It's the government; it's this and that, everything but not me!*

My life was a roller coaster of willpower, burnouts, and too much attachment. I always feared the worse, and many fears would manifest into physical reality! To escape, I had to put on more and more layers.

Do you want to design your life and business as a roller coaster? Are you seeking something to avoid pain? Do you want to hide all your life under the bed in a victim mode? If not, start taking mindful action from a place of love! Look forward to good things that will take place as a result of your actions.

Pleasure-based motivation is pure LOA, and it's where you stop escaping, and you start creating. You become the queen or king of your castle. You become powerful!

Pain-based motivation is taking action based on what other people want for you and trying to escape from that. Pleasure-based motivation is when you finally choose yourself, your dreams, and desires. Be yourself with no more layers. The more layers you get rid of at the beginning of your journey, the better. Taking action will feel so much lighter and so much meaningful.

Right now, I'm at the most creative and productive stage of my life. Yet, I put in fewer hours, have better outcomes, and more time for self-care and self-development. All because I'm no longer in this *escape the pain* mentality!

Why Full Responsibility Is Sexy and Attractive (and the Universe Will LOVE You for It!)

Another mindset shift you need to apply to move forward is being fully responsible for everything in your life. Release all old stories and excuses such as *I can't do this because I'm too old, too young, I'm a male, or female*. This is your old identity trying to stop you. It's your old self-image that defines your identity and, therefore your reality.

Where you are right now is the result of who you have been, consciously or unconsciously. Don't let any past failures define you! Even if you think you failed, in reality, you were learning and setting the foundation for your new, awesome reality.

There's no such thing as failing, you succeed, or you learn. My only regret now is that in the past, I didn't fail enough! I was so scared back then. Now, I no longer care about "failing." I take action from a place of curiosity. For example, right now, I'm testing a new business idea on the side. I completed a training program, studied it, and am taking action on it every evening. I enjoy the process of learning. I know that even if I don't get any quick results in terms of dollars made, the effort I'm putting in to learn more about marketing online will eventually pay off. I can see the bigger picture.

This is how all love-based leaders think; they invest in their skills but don't get too attached to a particular business opportunity.

But my old self would panic: *oh, what if it doesn't work, or maybe it's a scam, why does it always work for others, but not for me?*

Trust me when I say this: all your effort will be rewarded! Perhaps, you're creating content to attract clients, and things seem to be moving too slow. But think about your efforts this way: by curating quality content, you're adding value and collecting your good karma points. At the same time, you get on the vibration of extreme generosity! People will feel your good energy. Even if the sales don't come directly from the products or services you originally and logically designed to make revenue, your efforts eventually are rewarded.

When I first started on my writing journey, I made most of my books free. Many authors would laugh at me! I just kept writing and publishing all for free! But by being generous with my content, I attracted a following of loyal readers. Yes, some of those readers just wanted free eBooks and had no buying intention whatsoever, that's fine. But, one of my old readers who discovered me through my free content, and received value from it, began promoting one of my books to her following. This is how I achieved my first successful book launch!

Without spending money on any advertising! I knew I was using energy marketing. What you invest, you'll get. It may be a different channel or a different person. It may take longer. But it'll all come back to you if you stay patient and focus on creating value by authentic self-expression (more on patience later).

Everything has consequences. What you focus on expands! This is how quantum physics work. When you focus on what you don't have or what can go wrong, your life, business, prospects, clients, and employees will reflect that.

But when you allow yourself to take that quantum leap and think and act as your new self, it feels as if everything around you was designed to help you.

Trust me, a few months of identity shifting work can make remarkable changes in your life and business. When you start looking back at your old self, you'll be amazed at how long you've come!

Doubts and focusing on the negative makes you feel contracted. But when you switch your mindset to what could go well and all the fantastic things you can create, you feel joy. You're truly immersed in the process, and so there's no space for fear or doubts. There's only expansion!

Mindful Clarity for Magnetic Confidence (don't let your old self block you!)

Having clarity and moving with conviction and confidence automatically erases procrastination. You need to know your *why*.

-Why do you do what you do?
-Is it because you don't want to be mediocre, or is it because you want to be extraordinary?
-Is it to avoid being poor, or do you want to attract abundance?

The line between your old and new self is always very narrow, and you must be careful in every step you take. You don't need any specific meditations, just be mindful of your everyday routines, thoughts, actions, and the reasons why you take them.

Slowly but surely, start thinking and acting as your new self!

Now, if you're already in business, I assume you know your strengths, weaknesses, and your business model. But, if you're a new entrepreneur, and you're trying to figure out what kind of business to start, the following questions can give you some ideas *(at the end of this book, I also share practical information for different business models and ideas and further resources to help you).*

Mindful Clarity Exercise (know your why and your biz model like your life depends on it)

Do you envision yourself operating an online business you can run from your laptop so that you can travel the world and be location-independent?

Or perhaps you want an online business to work from home and spend more time with your family, friends, and loved ones?

Do you see yourself running an offline business, perhaps a small café, art gallery, or maybe a spa or a healing center?

Perhaps you can imagine the value you could create for your local community?

Or maybe you want to do both?

Do you coach clients? Where do you meet? Do you also offer online coaching?

What do you see yourself doing?

Be sure to envision it all from the first person.

Perhaps you'd like to get paid to be an international speaker, coach, or consultant. Can you see yourself traveling and speaking at different conferences? How would that feel?

Are you an introvert or an extrovert? Perhaps you want an online business that doesn't require talking to people at all?

Maybe you're a tech nerd or a marketing wizard, and you picture yourself building funnels and advertising campaigns for clients? Perhaps you build websites?

If you enjoy writing, maybe you're working on your own author brand? What do you write? Fiction, nonfiction, or both?

Maybe you write website content for clients? Or perhaps you're a grammar nerd, and you edit and proofread documents and books? What kinds of books and what types of documents?

Do you know foreign languages? How about offering a translation service for clients? Heck, you could even translate entire books in topics your passionate about. Imagine you get paid to translate Law of Attraction (LOA) books, wouldn't that be great?

If you love art and design, perhaps you run a print on demand business, you create different designs and upload to different websites to make a passive, royalty-based income?

Or maybe you create designs for clients or do branding services?

Perhaps you just enjoy buying and selling stuff online, well then how about starting your eCommerce business? Do you have your own online store? Maybe you also have your brand on websites such as Amazon?

You love coaching and healing; well, maybe you create transformational programs and online courses you can share with the entire world? Perhaps you also have a YouTube channel where you upload beautiful and inspirational videos?

Maybe you're a freelancer working with different clients and companies; well, what is your strength? What services can you offer to the world?

Do you think your current skillset is enough, or perhaps you'll need to gain more knowledge to become an expert? Will you need any certified courses or extra training?

Keep asking yourself empowering questions, and you'll find your answers!

Who do you work with? What kind of people do you attract to your business? What do you help them with? How do you interact with them? What do they tell you after you deliver your services and products?

Your imagination can be your best friend; this is where it all starts; use it to mindfully create, not to fearfully destroy.

What are you moving towards? Take full responsibility because nobody can write your destiny. You have your own unique path to follow; your energy is unique; you are unique.

Don't hide it; use it to your advantage by being authentic. In the current world, especially online, more and more people add more layers and want to present themselves in a superficial way. But I believe that now, more than ever, people need honest, authentic, and positive leaders. Be that leader, apply it as your motivation; the world needs you and your work!

Also, good, heart-led leaders understand it's not only about them, they understand their *why* and their *who*. Imagine you see an ad that says:

"We're hiring because our boss wants to buy a new Lambo!"

You would probably laugh, wouldn't you? But so many business owners operate from the "me, me me" mindset.

The "me me me mindset" also comes from a place of escaping from pain, and it's a short-term vision. Yes, of course, an owner of a well prosperous business has every right to buy things he or she wants, and there's nothing wrong with that.

But, as Zig Ziglar says, to get what you want, you must help other people get what they want. Those other people are your customers and can also be your team. Even if you're a solopreneur like me, at some point, you might be hiring a freelancer, independent contractor, or a professional service.

It's essential to have a vision and an infectious mission. For example, when looking for a proofreader for my books, I don't want just any proofreader; instead, I intend to attract a professional who also has a passion for LOA, spirituality, mindfulness, and small business.

That person is also an entrepreneur with her goals and vision, and I want to make sure she's happy editing my books. When people love what they do, they do a much better job, and everything just flows. It all starts with you and your inner leadership. Once again, you need to raise your standards and operate from your higher Self!

Revolutionary, heart-led businesses focus on the long-term. Their leaders always work on their passion and motivation muscle to transfer their vision to their teams.

How Curiosity-Based Mindset and Mindful Discipline Can Help You Manifest Faster (without stress or burnouts)

Know who you are, know what you want, and know who it's for, and you'll be successful beyond your wildest dreams. Yes, I can see questions from skeptical readers:

"But what if I hire someone and he or she doesn't do a good job?"

Well, you'll learn how to hire better next time. I've made many mistakes with hiring people in the past. The reason? My old self.

I was always so skeptical about everything; no wonder it would almost always manifest, I was an embodiment of skepticism.

When you see the world through such a lens, you automatically criticize almost everything. As a result, very few people want to be around you, let alone do business with you. Of course, too naïve isn't good either; balance is key.

The bottom line is, your mind works like a search engine. So, instead of asking yourself what could go wrong, ask yourself what can go well!

What if I hire an independent contractor, and he or she finishes this project earlier?

What if I publish this book and people like it?

What if I publish a video or a podcast, and it goes viral?

Train your mind for positive outcomes; even if they don't manifest now (there's always a time lag), eventually, they will. Every time you want to complain, focus on gratitude. Use curiosity to take action!

Curiosity-based action is something I learned from authentic marketing expert George Kao (I highly recommend you look him up on YouTube and Amazon).

Here's an example:

Let me launch this course and let's see how many people buy it this time!

Let me write 3 new blog posts every week to see what happens.

Let me just upload my first video to YouTube to see if maybe one person will watch it.

Sometimes, I like to use humor, and I ask myself:

Let's see how terrible this book can get?

Let's see how I can screw up this product launch?

Maybe it can be a good story I can share with other entrepreneurs at some point?

Once again, you don't fail. You succeed, or you learn! This is how you develop your mindful discipline muscle and create your own process. So many people take action only when they feel like it (especially in LOA/spiritual community). The opposite of that is too much hustle and grind (the entrepreneur community).

Personally, I like daily process-oriented goals and mindful discipline. For example, I write every day for at least 1 hour, no matter what. That allows me to write and publish new books regularly. It's who I am, and it's what I do.

A friend of mine is pursuing her goal as a motivational YouTuber. She still has a full-time job during the week.

Specifically, every Saturday, she records several videos in a row, and then edits, and uploads them to YouTube on Sunday. During the week, she works in a 9-5 job. Before going to her office, she works out, and after her 9-5, she coaches clients.

Her next goal is to have an assistant for tech-stuff and video editing, to free up her Sundays so that she can focus on creating programs and coaching clients. Then, she'll be able to fully shift into entrepreneurship.

It's all about creating your own process and following it! Even if it takes longer, it doesn't matter because the process alone helps you shift your identity and become the person you need to be to keep creating the life and business of your dreams!

Also, imperfect action and imperfect product or service that helps someone is much better than the perfect project that never gets launched and never helps anyone, right?

Inaction brings doubts, fear, and worry. Mindful action and discipline bring freedom and abundance. More importantly, they help you shift your identity and change your core. No advanced meditation or rituals are required. Just start taking action like your *New 2.0 Version* would! Be what you want to manifest and vibrate on the same level!

Releasing the Perfectionist Syndrome

Knowing how to manage your mind equals peace. Letting your mind control you, can equal stress. And, by the Law of Attraction, stress means contraction, not expansion. A stressed mind creates a stressed body. It's hard to think and make quality decisions when you're always stressed. You want to make your mind work for you so that you can move with grace and ease.

When you act under stress, you're trapped in a fear-based mindset, so, you take action to escape the pain rather than focus on pleasure.

Ask yourself, are you getting too attached to the final outcome? Do you put your work on the pedestal? Is there too much meaning you attribute to your business and brand?

I used to be guilty of all of the above until I understood that everything is constantly changing and becoming. So, what's the point of getting too attached to something that is moving? Imagine you tie yourself to a moving object hoping for security and peace of mind. Well, you'd get precisely the opposite.

In entrepreneurship, many people get too attached to the amount of money they make! *I'm a 6-figure entrepreneur; I'm a 7-figure consultant, or an 8-figure this or that.* Nothing wrong with that if your focus is on authentic expansion, growth, and reaching your full potential, in a way that you enjoy.

But, if you build your entire identity and happiness based on the amount of money your business makes, you ask for suffering. Any business is bound to have months of lower revenue and traffic. Something can happen. So, if all your source of accomplishment comes from attaching yourself to the result, any slight slip on your journey will result in anxiety or even lost motivation.

You are NOT your revenue, you are NOT your business, and you are NOT how many followers you have. See yourself as a powerful creator, and take pride in staying in motion and doing what's best for your vision. But don't define your entire being around your results.

I know an author who achieved terrific results with book publishing, especially audiobook publishing. The writer even reached a 6 figure a month number in sales. I could quickly tell he began building an ego around that accomplishment. There's nothing wrong with that, if a person truly wants to honor all the hard work he or she put in and that author worked really hard.

But the problem appeared when his major audiobook retailer changed their terms of service, and from one day to the next, his income was drastically cut down. Then, he totally lost his motivation and inspiration to create new books. Instead, he just complained on social media.

At the same time, many other authors found themselves in a similar situation: their income went down, but instead of complaining, they focused on publishing new books for their readers as well as building new ventures around writing and creativity.

The bottom line is – you need to learn how to go with the flow. Nobody can promise you that your success will last forever. I, too, had to learn it the hard way. Observe your reality and always do your best. If one opportunity comes to an end, another one will emerge. You need to master how to move forward. Don't turn around.

This is what I like to call the mindset of constant flow. And that mindset will also help you release the perfectionist syndrome! I'm still a recovering perfectionist. Chasing perfection would always paralyze me, and I was so scared to share my books with the world. Why? Because deep inside, I was attaching myself to the perfect but non-existent outcome.

My mind would constantly torture me with: *what if someone doesn't like your book, and he or she posts a negative comment?*

So, then I tried very hard to avoid negative thoughts. Here's the thing though, your subconscious mind can't process the "not" and "don't," so it hears: *yes, please, think negative thoughts.*

Then, you get yourself in a hypnotic trance, and you become unconscious. You think you're conscious because you go along with your day and whatnot. But, you're totally possessed by negative thoughts and paralyzed with fear.

If I tell you not to think about pink elephants, what will you see in your mind?

Yes, the pink elephant, how lovely!

Negative thoughts and "trying not to think negative thoughts" is such an energy drain. Then, you get angry with yourself, and you start *"should-ing"* yourself!

At this stage of my entrepreneur journey, I SHOULD be making this amount of money. Everyone on Instagram is successful, but not me. I SHOULD be this and that.

Such torture for your body, mind, and soul. And such an energy drain. Because all that energy we waste on fear, worry, *"should-ing"* ourselves, and trying to be perfect, can be spent on creating, growing, and expanding.

To escape this rather unpleasant cycle of negativity, find 1-3 activities that you know are good for you, help you center your mindset, and move you in the right direction. This can be reading or listening to someone who inspires you or immersing yourself in an activity that you know is good for you and your business (for example, learning a new skill, creating content, or customer avatar research).

Break those negative thoughts by taking positive and meaningful action!

Uncertainty and lack of ability to commit also lead to overthinking. This happens when a person buys a ton of business training programs, gets lost in the shiny object syndrome, and can't commit to one business model, to start.

So many new entrepreneurs chase different streams of income. Now, yes, diversification and different streams of income is a smart idea for a long-term vision. However, all businesses with different streams of revenue started with just one. It's not possible to grow so many things at once, especially as an inexperienced solopreneur. And when it comes to the Law of Attraction, what I found the most effective, is to focus on one manifestation at a time!

The main reason new entrepreneurs fear commitment to one business idea is that they get desperate to make something work ("escape the pain" motivation). While testing different opportunities is a smart idea, many beginners get lost in testing and jumping all over the place, never mastering one business model or venture.

What if I commit, but I don't get results fast? This is the fear-based mindset behind chasing the shiny object syndrome. But, once you switch your mindset to:

Let's see what I can learn from this opportunity/ business model, or: *let's determine if it aligns with my strengths and passions;* everything changes!

Don't be afraid to commit because all that effort eventually pays off. There's always something you learn on your journey! And what you learn, nobody can ever take away from you.

If you're a creative or content creator, you're probably not new to experiencing blocks. Or perhaps you think you're not good enough and should wait for more? Well, guess what? Had I stayed in that mindset, I wouldn't be writing this book now.

Assume readiness, peace, and abundance and move with certainty. The only cure for overwhelm is action. You've already arrived at your destination.

Do you want to be a writer? Write! This is what writers do; they write every day! Want to be an artist? Create! Don't worry about all those critics who never take any action, and all they can do now is criticizing what they can't do themselves. Be open to feedback, but only from people who are already successfully doing what you want to be doing and people you specifically create for (your audience and clients).

Your answers will unfold when you allow yourself to stay in motion!

From my experience, simple-minded people have it much easier than logical people. I've always been a very rational person myself. Not only that, I'd still focus on what could go wrong. I trained myself to be more simple-minded and not take myself and life so seriously.

Humor can help you keep going as well! For example, if you create content and get a nasty comment, celebrate it. Create a funny image in your mind, where you're on the stage giving awards to your most prominent critics:

Well done Ms. or Mr. Critic, but still, not as mean as it could have been! We'll be working hard to make sure you have enough of our new work to criticize and look forward to reading your application!

At the same time, be sure to focus your attention on positive comments and feedback and be thankful for all of them. Rome wasn't built in a day!

Be mindful of your favorite distractions and things you like to do to escape work that you know is your gate to impact and abundance. Let's say, you're a coach, and you promised yourself to do 3 live videos on your Facebook page every week.

But, you're still working a full-time job, and now you had a bad day, the boss was mean, and all you want to do is go home and indulge in watching Netflix and drink some wine to numb yourself.

Catch those thoughts when they come and break the pattern by doing something else, for example, play some funky music and dance around. Or think about some nice memory.

Then, get up, brush yourself off, keep your promise, and do those live videos. You're doing them not for you but for your people; you want to help them with your knowledge and expertise. Maybe they also had a bad day and need some uplifting content. Perhaps, they're even thinking of indulging in some kind of escapism but now they'll watch your inspirational live video and do something else. The next day they'll feel better and inspire those around them. Your actions always have a compound effect on your reality and other people's reality.

Also, nowadays, people want to connect with real people, not some perfect gurus.

So, be authentic and share. You had a bad day at work, but you're still doing your thing because you enjoy helping your audience. It's so much better than waiting for the perfect moment. Once again, it's not only about you; it's also about people you can help (and people they can help and inspire, directly or indirectly).

When you create from a place of honesty and vulnerability, something amazing happens, you become a magnet, and you naturally attract people who are on the same vibration. All you need to do is to show up and be yourself! Whatever it is you want to create, simply start creating!

Yes, at first, very few people might take an interest. But eventually, your efforts will compound. For example, nobody cared about my earlier books from 2017. It was only after I released *How Not to Manifest* and *Money Mindset*, that I began attracting a new audience of readers, and they began checking out my earlier work.

The Law of Attraction loves patience. It's like walking into your favorite restaurant and ordering your food. You understand you need to wait for it, and in the meantime, you can enjoy a nice cocktail or a glass of wine.

But now, in the era of the internet we live in an instant gratification mode!

Our ancestors had to move more than we do now, and they had to do it to survive. Now, we can get everything delivered to our door, we spend a lot of time on our devices, and as a result, all the excess potential doesn't get dispersed. Instead, all that extra energy accumulates in our minds. The more we think, the more paralyzed we get. Sometimes we seek escapism, which can even lead to addictions.

Besides staying in motion and combating fear by taking positive action, you can also move from your head to your heart!

Use Your "Who" to Get Out of Your Head

Your heart represents the joy of creating for others and helping them transform. Whenever I find myself too much in my head or am not too sure what to write about next, I talk to my readers, and I focus on their problems, challenges, and the transformations they want to experience.

You can also do it in your business, in multiple different ways, depending on your business model, for example:

-find a forum or Facebook groups related to the topic you teach and look for questions people ask, their problems and frustrations- whatever it is you create, make it your mission to help them.

-if you have an offline business, for example, a beauty salon, or a restaurant, start reading reviews online about similar establishments and see what their customers like and don't like so that you can create a service or experience based on that.

-if you sell physical products, on or offline, go to Amazon or other eCommerce sites, and read reviews people leave on similar products. Explore what's on their minds, what they want, and how your business can help them.

-if you're an artist or a creator, ask yourself, how do you want your audience to feel? What kind of emotion? Try to express that with your art.

Get out of your head and focus on what your customers want. Place your hands on your heart and say: *thank you for giving me the opportunity to serve you today.*

This is how you'll find your answers and solutions. A relaxed, peaceful state aimed at serving others! At the same time, it's also beneficial for your wellbeing, because you won't be so much in your head, and you'll have more energy to do the things you love. And if you like looking for answers in someone's head, be sure it's your ideal customers', not yours!

Whenever your mind suffers, your business suffers too, because you're unable to make good, empowered decisions and get stuck in the negative emotions of running away from the things you don't want.

Drive your mind away from identifying with what's changing, such as your revenue. Instead, focus on the pleasure of developing your mental and emotional muscles. Enjoy the game in itself!

Whatever Happens, It Happens FOR You!

Pain is merely an indication of danger. When you feel pain in your body, you know your body gives you feedback that something is out of balance. Suffering, however, is the pain of the mind that you can consciously inflict on yourself by focusing on the negative. Not everything is you. Don't identify with your car, house, income, and clients. Be mindful of the fact that thoughts alone are not dangerous, but they can grow into overthinking, and this is where you may get out of balance.

Things can always happen. A website you do your business on can change its policy. Your government can raise taxation. Advertising costs can go up. You can't change any of those events. But you can choose how you respond to them and how you use them to motivate yourself to keep creating and building.

As I'm writing this book, the world is still trying to come to terms with the post-lockdown reality. Many people were forced to start working from home. Some complained, but some saw this as an opportunity to finally learn online skills or change the way they worked. During the lockdown, some people focused on fear and complaining and that nothing was worth it anymore. In contrast, some used their time to learn how to start an online business, even though they felt fear of the unknown, and nobody could guarantee anything.

This is why the best entrepreneurs are courageous! Courage is when you take action despite fears and despite a lack of security or guarantees. As a matter of fact, the only guarantee you can get is the one you give yourself, to be yourself, and to do anything you can, right here at this moment.

Personally, I used the lockdown time to improve my health, energy, and mindset. I closed the business I was no longer passionate about. The pandemic affected it anyway, so I used it as a motivation to be honest with myself and moved on.

Then, I decided to focus entirely on writing. I knew that my mission of helping people raise their vibration was needed as never before.

I know many lightworkers who use different healing modalities, and they too used the global pandemic as their motivation to put their work out to the world, whether through their books, courses, coaching, or online workshops. It doesn't matter which vehicle you choose as long as it's aligned with your passion and strengths.

As an empath, I know that feeling the pain of others can sometimes be paralyzing. But, understand that the best thing you can do is to step into your inner leadership first. You were given your gifts for a reason, so don't hide them!

Many empaths get triggered by manipulative, sociopathic, or narcissistic people in power. They write long posts of complaints on their Facebook profiles. Why not use this creative energy to focus on the line of work that's the opposite of manipulation, and that inspires change? Have you noticed that megalomaniacs and narcissists are not usually afraid to put themselves out there? Even though they don't have anything good to offer to other people, it's all about them and their power and recognition.

Well, why not use that to motivate yourself to put yourself out there with your line of work and with your authentic self-expression to actually help people? Instead of complaining about governments and people in power, you don't like, govern, and empower yourself! Give yourself permission to lead and inspire others in a way that is empowering, all from a place of love.

Be the opposite of those narcissists! But, stick to the one thing you can learn from them; they aren't afraid to put themselves out there. They're consistent with their message. What about you and your message? You know it's positive; you know it can help people. Yet you worry about what will others think of you? Perhaps you fear doing Facebook live streams, because maybe one of your cousins will see what you do, and your family will start making fun of you?

Well, if that's the case, you can use technology to your advantage. Create another Facebook profile, only for your work and clients and use a different name for it (for example, add or get rid of your middle name). Then, block all your family and friends from that profile (so they will never see any of your work-related stuff, but you can still stay friends on your current profile that you can keep for personal interactions only).

How about that? Many people feel a huge relief, knowing that they can just do their own thing, and nobody from their family and friends will make any remarks. Of course, this can change; maybe your family and friends are very supportive and want to see you make live videos about energy healing or your coaching sessions. It's up to you! But yes, you can always have a personal and professional profile, nothing wrong with that.

And just as if you were running a shop or a restaurant, you can choose who you allow into your space. Any negative energy can be blocked.

It seems simple but so many beautiful coaches, lightworkers, creators, or authors put off their mission because they're too afraid of what someone in their family might say. Or perhaps they want to hide their humble beginnings.

Speaking of which, to be absolutely honest with you, I feel ashamed when I look at my old books. But, they're all a part of my journey! Had I not gotten started several years ago, I wouldn't have the courage to be writing this book.

Be true to yourself. Inner lies, just like all lies, are very short-legged and can only lead you to mental suffering. Don't be afraid to be who you were meant to be! Choose how you feel about yourself and the work you do. Combine spirituality with smart, action-based entrepreneurship, feminine energy with masculine energy, intuition with logic, desire with intention.

Use that energy in your learning and personal as well as business education. For example, study spirituality and psychology to get to know yourself and other people, but at the same time, study marketing and business to understand how to stand out, market yourself and make your message understood by your prospects and clients.

Most empaths, healers, and heart-led entrepreneurs are so scared of learning about business and marketing, and I've been there too! But once again, think about all those sociopaths and narcissists who get followed by some many people. They study business and marketing all the time; they know how to put themselves out there and have no shame.

Imagine if all heart-led entrepreneurs also used such a mindset but in a positive way. What if all our media suddenly get flooded with positive, love-based messages? While this vision is a bit idealistic, it's not impossible.

You see, to shine your light and embody the business you love, sometimes you will need to break the ice and do things that maybe you're not very passionate about. Remember when I told you how I fell in love with numbers and accounting? Now my life and business are so much better. And before that, it was impossible for me to focus on growth; I was way too *hippie woo-woo!*

At the same time, I know many great business people who could benefit from balancing out their masculine side by studying spirituality and incorporating more empathy and heart into their businesses.

Ask yourself which side you need to work more on? Your masculine or your feminine side? From my personal experience, I tested both extremes. At some point, I was a total embodiment of woo-woo and was just expecting daily miracles to come to me without doing anything. A cold awakening took place when I realized I was running out of my savings, had bills to pay, and no income coming in, and needed to take action to actually offer products and services that people can buy.

At the same time, I also experienced the opposite extreme when I was in a blind hustle mode, just hustling more, taking more action. It was all about me and my revenue, and even though, logically, everything was going well, at some point, I encountered burnout and a huge block, precisely as I described at the beginning of this book.

You can use identity shifting anytime and ask yourself whether you need to immerse yourself more in spirituality or business and marketing education or actions.

This is how you combine the Law of Attraction with the Law of Action. And this is what all well-known LOA gurus do themselves. They know how to do the inner work, and this is what they teach; but aside from that, they also run businesses, where they create products, and services that help people.

They don't rely on hoping to win the lottery. Instead, they design businesses they love because they understand that long-term success comes from taking meaningful action and having a purpose.

Oh, Elena sounds great, but I still have no idea what business to do! No idea where to start!

Well, first of all, let go of all that pressure. You can focus on the joy you experience as you go through finding out which business might be right for you or what you purpose is. At the end of this book, I included some resources from other authors as well as a few business ideas you can explore. Don't try to rush or start a business just because you feel like everyone is building one. Entrepreneurship is also about growing your mental and emotional muscles. So, if you still have no idea what to do, make it your mission just to be yourself, and focus on learning. Eventually, when you find the right idea, you'll know exactly what to do!

I had a friend, who's now a successful coach. People pay her large fees to get coached, and she has a long waiting list. But, it took her 8 years of exploration and constant testing of different ideas to find her purpose. Everyone would laugh at her and call her "a niche jumper" because she was all over the place. One week she was in a weight loss niche, then she was a Facebook ads marketer, then she was editing videos for other people, and then she was teaching meditation.

Yet she was on her mission to find her niche and ideal customer avatar; and when she did, she was almost an instant success.

Why? Because she was an all-in-1 woman, seriously! She knew how to do live videos to connect with her audience, set a blog, and write posts that ranked well in Google; she recognized how to run paid traffic ads on different platforms. She even understood what to eat to take care of her own health and manage her energy. She just kept testing different ideas and never gave up. And people who laughed at her, well, now they're on that waiting list, hoping to get accepted as clients!

Action leads to attraction!

How NOT to Learn (Avoid This Trap)

The mere passion for learning itself is priceless, even though many seasoned entrepreneurs lose it. It's because of the mainstream mindset ingrained by our society: you're supposed to know what you want to do until the rest of your life in your late teen yours to go to college and get an education to work the same job your entire life.

Nothing wrong with this scenario for people who already know their path. But, the best experts and professionals never stop learning. There's always something to explore, and it's never too late to change your profession as long as you have enough courage to learn and grow.

However, with learning comes one danger that I should mention. While pursuing more knowledge, we are tempted to go on social media and look for a guru. While there's nothing wrong with looking for an expert who can help you on your journey to mastering a new skill or modality, you must be very careful who you open your mind to.

The world of social media is full of hype, and many people, even though they may have good intentions, make posts about how great their lives always are. Some exaggerate or embellish their income or achievements. For example, instead of saying: *we have hundreds of satisfied students*, they say: *we have thousands of satisfied students.* Or they brag about their revenue, not profit. This can be very detrimental to an inexperienced entrepreneur!

You might find yourself thinking you're not good enough! Other people seem to have more free time, more travel, more freedom, more money, more love, and more impact. Everyone throws their perfect formula at you, amplified by some FOMO (fear of missing out) marketing technique.

Be very mindful of how much time you spend on social media and people you follow. For me, personally, I currently don't use social media, except for occasional use of my personal Facebook profile. I deleted all my other profiles over a year ago to immerse myself in inner work. So far, I don't miss social media at all.

But I do realize that for many of my readers, social media channels also serve to grow their business, and they can't just let them go. Well, in that case, use those channels as a powerful creator. Use inspiration and empathy instead of fear, bragging, and other manipulative tactics. Be an honest social media personality, and let that honesty become your personal reality. Like attracts like.

Many entrepreneurs talk about transparency and how honest they are, but their actions don't align with what they say…don't be that person. To create a true, authentic brand, your actions must align with what you say and think!

(yes, the Universe is aware of what's going on inside you).

Don't get hooked on social media scrolling and comparing yourself to other people. You compare yourself to others, you get bitter, you compare yourself to yourself yesterday, and you get better! Social media is designed as a quick fix. You just must click on that video and watch it!

Social media platforms can drain your creative energy. I can't even tell you how many times I had ambitious plans to start writing and decided to check Instagram real quick. Before I knew it, I was on someone's webinar, ordering a course I didn't really need. I should have just focused on writing!

This is why, for now, I don't use social media; I have more time for self-care, writing, and inner work. It works well for me! But if you use social media, use them in a mindful way to connect with people you want to connect with or as a platform to share your message and grow your brand in an authentic way. Just be very aware of how you manage your time. Are you in a consumer or creator mindset? As an entrepreneur, your main focus should be creating, not consuming.

Finally, remember that most gurus on social media, can't go on a journey for you because it's your journey. You need to be your own guru. You already have all the answers you need. It's just the matter of asking yourself the right questions. One of them is: *what's my next step?*

Even when you follow a program that's a proven system, remember that it's just the first step. Eventually, for everything you do in life you want to have your own system; in other words, you need to have your own recipe for success.

Learning from other people is great; it can open your mind, and it can help you grow faster. But remember that you, your life, your customers, and your business are your best teachers!

Be your own guru; listen to your inner voice. Sometimes, stillness, a nice hike in nature, listening to soothing music, or meditating can be better than watching the latest guru's webinar desperately hoping it'll fix your life.

Also, don't lose yourself in learning as a way to escape taking action and practicing your skills. Just like with driving, you have to get in a car and drive, and just like with swimming, you must allow yourself to get into the water and swim.

Too much social media, as escapism or constant need for new information, can make you feel busy; you get this illusion that you're productive, and you're doing something. You get a dopamine hit; you experience a temporary high. Then you think about the things you wanted to do for your business and realize you're too tired to take action.

The Real Secret Behind Mindful Learning (hidden dangers of social media)

When it comes to learning, there's organized, intentional learning and chaotic, escapism-based learning. The first one is when you mindfully realize what skill you need to improve to attract certain results in your business. For example, you realize you need to hire a virtual assistant. So, you search for information or training on how to do this. Then, you proceed to hire and this is how you learn even more- by doing.

The second type of learning is more of a distraction than real learning. It's when you just want to keep your mind busy and watch random videos to kill time. Frequently, you may find yourself thinking you're not good enough. You see someone's content that says: *hey, why you're not manifesting a 7-figure business yet?* Then, you see another video of someone traveling the world, and you're wondering if your current business model is a good idea because perhaps you could make more money by doing something else. You feel guilty, chaotic, and disorganized, and so your business, clients, and whole reality begin to reflect that erratic feeling eventually.

Protect your mind!

Stimulation overload can also lead to anxiety. Then you feel guilty you're not taking action, you try to force yourself to be productive, and you end up feeling burned out. Then you start looking for something to get rid of anxiety, without realizing that it's your mind and actions that create it.

Try a social media detox! If you need social media for your business or any professional activity, be sure to separate your work profiles from your personal profiles. Delete social media apps from your phone so that you can't be scrolling. Anytime you feel like scrolling on your device, use it to read something positive instead. I know so many people who complain they'd love to read more, but they spend at least 1 hour a day scrolling on social media without any apparent purpose. That time can be spent on creating something meaningful, reading, or self-care. After quitting social media, I have more free time, and my mind is more peaceful. I hardly ever feel anxious now.

And if I do, I know it's because of overstimulation or a sudden influx of negative thoughts. Be careful where your focus goes, and anxiety won't get you.

I always say- stop scrolling and start manifesting!

All that scrolling time can be spent on positive thoughts and actions. You also keep your mind clean; there are no negative thoughts such as: *oh I'm not good enough, because other people on social media have it better, they're smarter, richer, fitter, slimmer, or* whatever.

Well, what you see on social media is never the whole picture. Many influencers don't want to share their bad days or mistakes. They also have their own gurus they follow while probably getting stuck with negative thoughts such as: *I'm still not good enough; I need more followers.*

It's a very vicious cycle!

Why keep yourself stuck in a prison of your own mind? Why wake up every morning with that heavy feeling in your chest?

What do you choose? Chasing something that's ideal and perfect but unreal? Or something that's imperfect but authentic and can help you grow long-term?

All your actions have consequences and all your actions compound. It took me 3 years of using social media every day to realize how my bad choice influenced so many decisions in my "old life." All those decisions were based on chasing something outside of myself, and escaping from what I didn't want, instead of focusing on what I truly wanted.

Take some time now and ask yourself what and who influences your decisions? Is it your new 2.0 self? Or is it your old self, deluded by some superficial images and posts on social media?

Do you seek approval from other people? Do you create to fit in? Or do you create because it aligns with what the 2.0 version of yourself would do?

Take a few minutes, close your eyes, take a few deep breaths. Align yourself with your new identity. What new empowering decisions can you make today to be in control of your mind tomorrow?

Success is a Relaxed State (Stop Contracting and Start Expanding)

Whenever you're feeling stressed, or anxious, or simply want to reach a deeply relaxed state, to feel better, make better decisions, and be a better leader, I highly recommend you try the progressive relaxation technique.

Progressive Muscle Relaxation by Edmund Jacobson

First, find a quiet place where you won't be disturbed. You can lie on the floor, bed, yoga mat, or just recline in a chair if you prefer.

Be sure to feel comfortable - if necessary, take off your shoes and loosen up your belt or tie.

Also, remove your glasses.

Rest your hands in your lap or on the arms of the chair while focusing on deep relaxation.

Now, take a few deep breaths, very slowly. Feel your belly moving as you breathe in and out.

Keep breathing as you gradually focus your attention on the different areas of your body.

Your Forehead:
Mindfully squeeze the muscles in your forehead, for about 15 seconds.

Feel your muscles becoming tighter.

Now, slowly release the tension in your forehead while counting for 30 seconds.

Can you feel the difference in how your muscles feel as you relax?

Continue to repeat this process several times so that your forehead feels completely relaxed.

When you feel your forehead is relaxed, move on to other parts of your body.

Your jaw:
Tense the muscles in your jaw, and hold the tension for 15 seconds.

Now release the tension slowly for 30 seconds.

Once again, notice the beautiful feeling of relaxation and continue to breathe slowly. Repeat several times if needed.

Your neck and shoulders:

(This one is my favorite as I always accumulate lots of tension in my neck).

First, increase the tension in your neck and shoulders by raising your shoulders toward your ears and hold for 15 seconds.

Slowly release the tension as you count for 30 seconds. Notice the tensions gradually dissipate.

Your arms and hands:
Slowly draw both hands into fists. Pull your fists into your chest and hold for 15 seconds, squeezing as tight as you can. Then gradually release while you count for 30 seconds. Recognize the deep feeling of relaxation.

Your Buttocks:

Slowly increase tension in your buttocks over 15 seconds. Then, slowly release the tension over 30 seconds.

Notice the tension alleviating. Be sure to breathe slowly and evenly.

Your legs:

Slowly increase the tension in your quadriceps and calves over 15 seconds.

Squeeze the muscles as hard as you can. Then gently release the tension over 30 seconds. Take note of the tension leaving and embrace the feeling of relaxation.

Your Feet:

While breathing deeply and slowly, focus on increasing the tension in your feet and toes.

Now, tighten the muscles as much as you can.

Slowly release the tension while you count for 30 seconds. Notice all the stress disappearing!

Continue breathing slowly and evenly.

Do this exercise whenever you feel stressed out. The truth is- if your body is relaxed, your mind will follow. When you relax, your visualization practice will take a new dimension; and, as a bonus, you'll feel great!

Relaxation can help you quickly rise above your "normal" state and reach new levels of awareness. It also blocks worry, impatience, and anxiety.

The Honest Truth about the Patience Muscle (use it to your advantage)

As I consciously began expanding my manifestation practice by expanding my state throughout the day, I realized one enlightening thing.

There's always a delay in results, and we need to work on our patience.

In other words, if it takes longer; at first, you may feel like you're wasting your time. This is what was happening in my life.

But what I learned is that thanks to visualizing and relaxing, my state improved, and so did my productivity.

I no longer felt overly attached to the result, I could finally enjoy the process, and from there, really amazing things began manifesting in all areas of my life. It was literally like a dream come true!

Ask yourself, how do your heart, belly, and throat feel? Do you notice anxiety or any contracted energy there? Close your eyes, visualize your dream reality, always from a first-person, always through your eyes.

Take a few deep breaths. Apply the relaxation technique I shared above whenever you notice any construction in your body, and continue your visualization.

Trust the process, hold your vision, and remember that the Universe is infinite intelligence; it already knows your order. However, let go of your specific ways and channels you predict your desire to manifest. It may be delivered in a different way than you thought, and that's OK!

The Universe may want to test you as well. Perhaps before you manifest your millions, it wants you to experience several bad investments and "failed" businesses?

Only because it wants you to practice for the bigger show! So that when you finally manifest your millions, you'll know how to stay away from bad investments and unprofitable business ideas. The Universe knows your path and the specific lessons you need to learn.

Don't fluctuate your state because you still can't see your dreams manifest in physical reality as fast as you wanted. Your dreams already exist, and your higher Self is already living them. So, focus your mind and heart on that! And feel good and relaxed in the present moment. Be aware of your mind and body. Negative states are just feedback. You can only be a witness of your thoughts, and mindfully ask yourself, who thinks this? Is it my old self or my new self? How does my new self think?

Now, at this stage, I'm pretty sure some readers are thinking: *how come she hasn't given us any strategy yet, any proven LOA protocol to follow?*

OK, do you want one?

Visualize for 7 minutes at 5:55 AM every morning, meditate for 17 minutes at 11:11 AM, and do your affirmations stating you're rich every day between 1- 3 PM. How's that for a protocol you can blindly follow because I told you to do so? I'm sure some readers are laughing!

As an entrepreneur, you need to learn to filter information and create your own systems and protocols. *The Law of Attraction for Entrepreneurs* and identity shifting isn't something you just do for 5 minutes every day. It's something you adapt as a lifestyle and play it as a game. Right now, you're reading this book, so ask yourself: *who reads it, is it my old self or my new self? Am I reading it to escape mediocrity or to align myself with excellence and abundance?*

It's not about sticking to any specific LOA ritual, although you can do your favorite rituals if you feel like it. For example, if you have any affirmations you like, use them! If you have a vision board that reminds you of your why, use it! There's no set way of doing any of those things. The best way is *your* way!

I know people who manifest amazing things, yet they never used any specific manifestation method. The only thing they do is identity shifting. They promise themselves to be their new, 2.0 self who is naturally grateful (doesn't have to try to be grateful), naturally positive (doesn't have to try to think positive), and is a natural manifester in a state of flow (doesn't have to try another method, to see that maybe, perhaps it'll work).

Play it as a game. Do you drink coffee? Well, have your next cup of coffee as your new self. Let's say you drink your coffee, and you catch yourself thinking your old limiting thoughts such: *oh, after paying all those taxes, will I be able to pay my bills? When will I be able to finally travel and live the laptop lifestyle?*

There's truly nothing wrong with that; these are normal thoughts of survival, so don't try to fight them. Just have your next sip of coffee, and allow yourself to think like your NEW self, make it into a game: *wow, I finally made it, and I can still remember how last year I'd drink coffee worrying about the bills to pay. Well now my only worry is to build an excellent team to work for me because I can easily afford it!*

Do you find yourself struggling to get up early? You can think like your old self, as someone who isn't an early riser and is trying to force themselves to be up early. Or you can take the driver's seat, step up into your new 2.0 version, and think thoughts such as*: I love being up early; nothing feels as good as getting my most important stuff done before breakfast! Now I have so much time for planning and growth.*

How about affirmations? Do you choose to be a person who feels poor and hopes to attract abundance while reciting some affirmations they don't even resonate with? *Maybe this will work because someone online is using it, and my new guru says it's the only way.*

Or, do you choose to think and feel like an abundant person who uses affirmations as a reminder of how awesome their reality is and how grateful they feel? You have the freedom to use any affirmation you want. Just be mindful of what sets you on fire.

For example, some people like words such as "abundance," or "freedom." But others prefer "money," "wealth," "wealth creation," or even "cash". Everyone is different, so there's no right or wrong.

What about vision boards? Do you tend to stare at yours, hoping that maybe one-day all those images come true if you try harder to manifest? Or do you look at all those fantastic images as your new, 2.0 version of yourself while feeling deep gratitude?

Imagine your business is offered a large sum of money. Let's say that in one day, you can receive what you made in the last 10 years, all in one day. Your old self may think:

Oh, *that's a lot of money, what will I do with all this money, what if I lose it?*

All those thoughts cancel LOA. But your new self can think:

It's normal for me to receive large amounts of money, I'm used to making this amount of money in 1 day. Everyone around me is doing it; it's just my reality. It's absolutely normal for me!

The Biggest Business Asset You Can Create (all great leaders have it!)

My old self would get really upset whenever I couldn't manifest fast:

Why is it taking so long? I work hard, I want to help people, and I invest in myself.

Well, it's not about the lack of effort, many people take massive action and don't get the desired results, and they don't know what's going on. It's seems something internal preventing their success from manifesting fast.

Well, you have to allow the process to take place.

That means patience. Now you can't say you're patient but complain at the same time. If you keep saying: *well, I've been waiting patiently, but I'm still not manifesting, it's not fair.* It means you're not patient.

The mere fact you're saying this proves to the Universe that there's no faith. You're basically blocking it yourself by lacking real patience. It doesn't matter what you say; it's more about who you are as a whole.

Yes, it can be frustrating; you take action, create, do everything you can and nothing happens.

And yes, of course, you can't just sit down and wait. So well done on taking action.

But have a look inside; if you keep saying you're patient and committed, but then you complain, you're not patient. Keep taking action and learning but have faith that at the same time, the Universe will arrange the divine timing. Also, in some cases, please note that some ventures may simply not be for you.

For example, I used to desire the social media influencer lifestyle because I saw other people do it. I worked hard on it, but it wasn't working out successfully. In the end, I realized such a model wasn't authentic for me. And because of that, I finally found my true calling, writing books.

So, there are two possible outcomes, you'll succeed eventually while building all your mental and spiritual muscles, or you'll discover that the venture wasn't for you. Still, in the end, you'll find out what to do to manifest your business success.

Let's say you created 50 videos on your social media profiles and are still not attracting the clients you want, or not the right kind of clients.

You begin complaining. Well, what signal do you send to the Universe? You don't have what you want, and so you complain. By your wish, the Universe will pick on your vibration and will amplify on it so that you keep attracting what you don't want.

Now, even if you hire a good business coach but are still operating from the vibration of lack, chances are you'll find a way to sabotage your success.

By focusing on what's going wrong, you create an emotional and vibrational memory of lack. Most people are very good at this, actually! I used to be very good at this too, but then I realized I could use the same skill but positively. I can create an empowering memory instead and stop complaining.

Trust me when I say this...some people may be on a low income. Still, they're so grateful and feeling so abundant inside that eventually, they start attracting wealth creation opportunities (if they choose so). At the same time, I know people who may be making a lot of money, but deep inside, they feel poor or not good enough, and so they start creating more and more of that feeling. In the end, it's all about your emotional bank account. And your emotional bank account loves patience.

Patience is when you create from a space of already having what you want. First, accept your wish in your mind. Create a positive memory of your dream reality now. Have faith that everything is coming at the right time! Trust the divine timing.

The obstacles come because the timing is not right, you're not patient, or something better is in store for you. It's just that your current state of awareness can't see it yet.

Why Coming Up with Your Perfect Client Avatar is NOT Enough Until You Do This One Thing!

All businesses want to attract quality clients; clients that are ready to work with them and can pay for products and services. Many entrepreneurs start with a dream client avatar, which is a brilliant thing to do. Clarity and specificity is everything. But, by the laws of the Universe, you don't always attract what you want. You attract who you are. So, if you, as a business owner, have limiting beliefs about money, are afraid to commit, invest in yourself and learn, chances are you'll be attracting clients and prospects who think in a very similar way.

Then, by the law of being reactive, you'll start complaining that it's hard to find clients, and your clients will complain it's hard to find quality services they want. It represents the perfect recipe for creating negative loops and feeling stuck.

In terms of attracting the right clients, ask yourself who you are and how you think. Do you think and act like a desperate business owner? Do you always try the latest marketing hack to find affluent people, assuming that just because they have money, they'll want to hire you?

(this is how I used to think and act, by the way! But my energy wasn't aligned to affluence, and so I'd attract affluent prospects and then repel them because of my old, desperate energy).

Your prospects, clients, business partners, and all people involved in doing business with you are a reflection of you!

An acquaintance of mine who is a spiritual coach complained a lot about unreliable clients. She told me how they would book free consults with her and wouldn't show up on those calls, and if they did, they only wanted to pick her brains without ever hiring her. Or those clients who did hire her wouldn't take action and didn't want to do any of the inner work exercises she'd give them. Some would ask for a refund while halfway into her programs.

At some point, she got interested in writing and publishing her own book, so she reached out to me for help. I recommended some books and training programs I'd taken to learn about book publishing, but she said she didn't have time and would love private coaching with me instead. Now, even though coaching is not something I normally do, since I liked the work she was doing, I offered to help her.

I put in lots of time and effort to study her brand, and came up with ideas for her book. I even created an outline of ideas to help her. She seemed committed at first. But, we scheduled a call, and she didn't show up. We scheduled another one, and she didn't show up again. Finally, she told me she needed 2 more months to have more time and money, and then she'd fully commit and pay for my services; she wanted to go all in.

So, I created a full outline for her and a detailed plan to write her book step-by-step.

2 months passed, and she stopped replying to my messages.

I don't mention this to judge this person! Because at some point, I was just like them, and no wonder I couldn't attract quality clients. It also became obvious to me why this woman would always attract clients who were not serious, wanted to pick her brains, and wouldn't commit. She was attracting who she was.

The bottom line is, any change you need to make in your business, starts with You! It's not about the latest online marketing hack; it's not about which social media platform is better.

(Although these strategies and technologies can be helpful, and we need some of them in this day and age.)

It's all about you and who you are. Be a serious business person, and you'll then attract serious clients.

Law of Attr-Action for Entrepreneurs

Use Energetic Micro Niche Marketing to Manifest Your Dream Customers with Ease

Now, as soon as you start changing yourself and get back to the root of the problem, you can focus on the next step, which is simple, honest marketing. Yes, be honest with who you want to work with or attract to your products and services.

In my case, I'm in an LOA space. However, as you may have noticed, I take a bit of a contrarian approach to most LOA gurus out there, so I make it very clear who my books are not for. In my author bio, book descriptions, and book intros, I tell people that I can't help them manifest an instant lottery win. I also mention that my books are for people who are ready to dive deep and work on their mindset and energy.

But when I first got started, I didn't know much about energetic marketing, and I was in a very naive mindset - I wanted to attract everyone who was interested in LOA. No matter who they were or what they thought, I intended to help everyone with everything! And so, my messaging was very scattered and too generic.

Because of that, I attracted many people who were still in a victim mindset and were expecting me to fix them in 7 seconds or less by giving them some LOA hack.

So, I learned my lesson, and I decided to re-brand my books, just by making it clear who I write for and who I don't write for.

Your energy should be spent on building a business you love so that you work with people you love and people you can help. When diving deeper with your who, don't just think about their gender, demographics, or interests. Ask yourself how those people think, what they feel, and what their desires are?

And yes, I had to learn it the hard way, but you can't help everybody. Personally, I'm a big fan of what I like to call energetic micro niches. In my case, LOA is a niche and a very big one. My mini micro niche is LOA for entrepreneurs, creatives, professionals, empathic healers, teachers, and leaders. People who want to use universal laws to add value to the world, make it a better place, and manifest abundance in all areas of their lives. I attracted you because you ARE that person!

Ask yourself what your energetic micro-niche could be and how you can bond with your ideal client avatar. The first step is to be yourself. Get rid of all those layers. Create and attract from a place of true authenticity.

The Total Immersion Formula to Eliminate Limiting Beliefs on Autopilot

What are your true dreams, goals, and ambitions? Are you separating yourself from them or getting closer to them?

It was only recently that I began to realize very specific patterns behind all my successes. My discovery led to a straightforward conclusion- whenever I could just focus on taking aligned action, and love the process without overthinking the result, concentrate entirely on the process, and immerse myself in the taste of my goal and vision; I could manifest not only faster but also with ease.

I also realized that it's linear thinking that most people apply, which doesn't always lead to success. Linear thinking is usually embodied by the following:

-I'm this, but I'm not good enough.
- I must set up these goals to be good enough like a person who has already achieved it.
-I need to torture myself to accomplish this goal, and only then will I be worthy of it.
- I want to be like my guru, so I'll try to do what they did- heck I am not good enough.
—My progress is too slow...I need to think logically what to do...etc.

This can be a never-ending rat race.

First of all- you're already good enough. All you want to do is re-launch yourself and create a new 2.0, or 3.0 or whatever version of yourself that you need right now so that it's aligned with your current goals. The current version of you aligns with your old goals and old vision. There's no good and bad, better or worse.

When you immerse yourself in the process of doing something, there's no place for self-doubt.

Also, for long-term success, you need to have a goal that excites you and the process you can control. You may not always control the end result; sometimes it may take longer to get exactly where you want to be. But when you focus on the process and forget about anything else, it'll be much easier.

Now, compare it to taking action with a negative mindset like:
-I am not good enough so I need to put on layers and pretend I'm someone else.
-Other people have it easy, but I don't.
-Other people have this and that.
-Other people do it faster.
-I'm ashamed to ask for feedback because I'm not good enough yet.
-I need to start that goal again.
-I never achieve my goals.

Such thinking can lead to a bunch of negative weeds in your head; and so, in the end, you feel paralyzed. I've been there too many times. Usually, because the goal was not for me, or, I had very unrealistic expectations, or I wasn't willing to fully immerse myself in the process and live it and breathe it. Taste your goal before you're ready. Use all your senses, and when you set a goal, don't just use your mind and logic but also your feelings and emotions.

Instead of overcomplicating things with: *"oh, first I need this and that and then I need to go there and do this"*, ask yourself: *"how can I taste it or even partially taste it?"*

My goal is to warmly encourage you to have a look at your situation, and your current goal, something that is in your heart, something you feel really is for you. Ask yourself:

-am I postponing my happiness and fulfillment in business and life?

-am I overplanning and overcomplicating the process?

-is there a simple way to at least taste my goal or my ideal lifestyle?

Even, if you can't afford something fully, there's always a way to taste it and plant this seed in your mind- you're worthy and confident enough to get what you want...

Your goals must come from you and excite you, don't get excited by someone else's plans if they don't align with your vision.

You need to taste your goal and vision in some way or another so that you are able to fuse yourself with them. Yes, you can do affirmations and visualize, but if it's just an automatic repetition and you don't feel anything, it won't be sufficient.

Chances are you want to repeat someone else's goal that isn't for you. Focus on the process without freaking out about the result.

For example, if your goal is to start a YouTube channel, set a simple process goal of doing one video a day because this is how you'll learn. You can start with a smartphone and later as you go, invest in better equipment; proper lighting, and camera. As long as you talk about something that adds value to someone (even if you're not perfect and not good on video), you can do YouTube. With each video, you do and upload, you will learn the mechanisms of this specific platform.

The total immersion makes you locate all your precious energy on the process. And by doing that really amazing things begin to happen:

-you don't have the time to think about other people and what they think about you.
-you don't have the time to torture yourself and your mind with the news or information that doesn't serve you. You're fully away from gossip, whether it's on or offline, and there are no toxic influences in your life.
-you become a passionate creator and see your process of acquiring skills that you'll always be able to apply somewhere else.
-you develop your emotional muscles.
-while you do have specific goals and vision in mind, you also understand that true success, happiness, and fulfilment comes from the unity of heart and mind.

Think about a project, you're postponing right now. Or a personal goal that somehow connects to your business or career.

- What is it? And what's holding you back?
-Did you even start? If you did, then what happened?

-How would your life change if you could get started in the next 7 days and move forward and finish faster?
-What's the number one thing that's holding you back?

Now, think about it, what's better...Something imperfect that helps people or something that was supposed to be perfect but was never created..?

I could indulge in thoughts like: *who am I to be writing this? I'm not Tony Robbins. I'm not a guru! What if I publish my work and someone doesn't like it?*

I always get annoying thoughts like these; the only difference is- with my current mindset, I can still take action.

I say to myself- *OK, that's why I need to do it. I need to show my inner demons that I'm in charge!*

Just break it down into a small action plan and focus on one step at a time and solve problems and obstacles as they come.

If all my attention goes into *what ifs* and negativity, I'll probably end up hiding under my bed, and I'll never do anything.

So, let's see what happens if you focus too much on the end goal...

Let's say you've uploaded one of your first videos on YouTube, and you start complaining: *oh, but it doesn't rank very well...I've only received 50 views*!

But then, when you really think about it and choose the positive mindset:

50 views is a lot! Imagine you are speaking in front of 50 people. That is quite an achievement. And you just shared your message with 50 people.

The same premise applies to bestselling authors. You'd be surprised that for most authors, it took dozens of books to actually learn the game of becoming a bestselling author.

Most people love instant success stories and overnight successes. Very few want to hear about the process and behind the scenes efforts. But, the truth is, that you become an "overnight success" after many years of aligned action. That aligned action can be fun!

Create Awesome Process-Based Goals (No More Anxiety!)

If you start comparing yourself with other people (unless you look up to them for inspiration, which is a different story), you'll likely mess it up before you start.

Example: you can set up a goal to reach 1 k subscribers on YouTube in 1 month.

Technically, it would be possible for someone who already has experience with the YouTube platform.

And of course, such a person has a process and a system in place.

However, a newbie, who sets up a goal of 1 k subscribers on YouTube in a 1 month time, might upload a few videos, get discouraged, and think: *but it doesn't work*. He or she then loses confidence, and motivation.

A better solution would be to set a goal like:
-Create 5 quality videos a week and upload them.
-Next, have a look at which videos get the most traction, optimize them, and get feedback from someone with YouTube experience
-Then, create systems that allow generating content faster (perhaps you can hire an assistant who could edit and upload your videos?)

Mindful Confidence is acquired by focusing on what we can control and mastering those skills.

Similar to a goal such as- write a book and make it an Amazon bestseller in 1 month.

This goal is easy and doable for someone who has experience with writing and publishing.

But someone who's new to writing, organizing content, working with editors and proofreaders, creating titles, hiring good designers, marketing, etc. will need more time. Hence, it makes more sense to build a solid foundation and focus on the process.

Process forms part of a vision that you have (such as certain number of followers or readers). Focus on what you can control and keep getting closer to that vision while becoming more confident.

Total Freedom from "What Will Other People Think of Me?"

Do you ever feel like you could do more, create more, and even have some specific ideas, but you tend to get stuck? You become totally blocked by fretting about what other people will think of you. Or perhaps, you move forward with your goals but deep inside, you know you could be moving faster and with more ease if you could just get rid of those annoying thoughts:

"What will other people think of me?"

This step is designed to give you freedom from that. It'll take some work and practice of course, but once you have ingrained it into your mindset, you'll feel so liberated!

I spent a lot of time obsessing about what other people thought of me. And then, obsessing about how to get rid of that annoying and disempowering feeling.

The real freedom came with acceptance. It's normal that some people may judge you. But it doesn't matter. If you concentrate on other people, your energy and focus will start suffering.

Also, what you may not be realizing is that there are many people who talk about you, because you inspire them, and they wish you well. So, focus on that.

Every second, minute, hour, the day is important in your mission. As an entrepreneur, you get to help other people and create abundance for yourself via your ventures. All your energy should be put into that thought and feeling.

You need to be mindful that there will be many forces that will try to distract you, and those forces may be in you, I call them-inner demons—all those voices in your head.

It's tough to get rid of all the negative feelings. But you can talk to them and handle them.

Example:

"I feel anxious about starting that service. I'm not a big company. What if nobody calls me? What if I waste my time setting it up and I don't get any clients"?

Just accept those negative thoughts because they want to tell you something.

Some negative thoughts can be transformed into positive action. Yes, you're not a big company, but it's not required to get started. All big companies got started as small ventures.

So, what can you do today to get started?

Once you have understood that, the next concept to dive into is your limiting beliefs. We all have them.

Many of those limiting beliefs are acquired from people you surround yourself with.

For example, if all your friends complain about their jobs and establish the mindset that it's just the way it is and that entrepreneurship is way too risky, will it make it easier for you on your journey as an entrepreneur?

On the other hand, if you surround yourself with ambitious people who have goals, dreams, desires, and pursue a different lifestyle, you'll be exposed to different energy, and you'll feel understood.

In the first scenario, it could be like talking to the wall, the wall of negativity. In the second scenario- it's hanging out with people who empower you and encourage you to go to the next level.

Some people are negative, but it's not their fault because they never had a chance to learn that there are ways to improve their mindset, lifestyle, and career. They never had access to any of that information. Or perhaps, they had negative experiences with entrepreneurship, got a limiting belief about it, and are passing it on as their way to "protect" other people.

What you need to realize are your limiting beliefs- and again, self-awareness and acceptance are so key!

For many, many years, I had a ton of negative beliefs about money, business, and marketing. It took me lots of work and research to gradually change my mindset towards an abundance mindset, and I'm still working on it.

If you're like me and you weren't born into a wealthy family, and you saw your parents work very hard yet they couldn't afford much, chances are you got limiting beliefs from them. It's not your family's fault; they tried the best they could and worked hard. Never blame other people.

What I find more powerful is this mindset: *in my family, everyone worked hard, and it's great because I learned the value of action!*

Why Strategy Isn't Enough (the Invisible Force of Self-Image)

It all starts with your self-image. If deep inside you think you aren't good enough or don't deserve something, it doesn't matter how many strategies you know.

For instance, I know people who know a lot about a ton of different diets, but they can never lose weight. The same applies to an online business. I've met so many people who know a ton of different online marketing strategies yet can never apply them to create lasting success. Something always goes wrong, and so they jump into learning another strategy.

Whatever it is that you want, wanting isn't enough. I'd even dare to say, taking action may not be enough if the action is random and not taken from a place of confidence.

With the wrong mindset, a person who takes action and fails usually gives up and creates an image of failure. At the same time, a person with a good self-image and confident mindset sees the whole experience as a lesson to grow and expand.

Different situations can be reframed.
Example:

I screwed up launching a product or a service. It didn't go as planned.

I have 2 choices:
1. This isn't for me, I'm not talented, it's too much work, and I'm not good at marketing.

2.I learned a lot about the business that's awesome. Now, I can do it again with a better process.

Never let bad memories make you feel unworthy of success. What you assume about yourself, you project it onto other people who also pick it up.

That doesn't mean you have to lie about who you once were or be inauthentic. You start by accepting yourself and who you are and use that as motivation and starting point for full transformation.

But remember, you have the freedom to become who you want to become.

Don't make your goals smaller; make your self-image better and more aligned with your big vision.

Empowerment exercise:
-How do you look at yourself?
-What are the emotions you felt when you were successful?
-What are the 3 things you're manifesting right now?

The ONE Exercise You Must NEVER STOP Doing!

We always visualize. And we always create our reality. But, whether it's our dream reality, is a different story!

Most people just run on autopilot, between careers they hate and self-imposed distractions to entertain themselves in between.

This is why it's so important to make our minds work for us, not against us. It's vital to design your ideal day in your mind and write down all the details.

Believe it or not, I used to be very skeptical about it. For many years, I'd say: *just show me how to make more money and then, I will be able to feel good and do whatever I want! This inner work is all BS!*

At some point, I disconnected from myself and forgot about my why and my vision. All days were busy and stressful. Friendships were rare and very superficial. Then I realized that I created a reality that was a prison, not freedom.

So, I got back to doing the ideal day exercise...

It may be a bit challenging at first; perhaps you'll find yourself thinking: *oh, but I don't really know what my ideal day looks like.*

But as long as you sit down every day, and write down the details of your ideal day and try to feel them, live them, and focus on the positive emotions you experience, you will be able to unblock yourself.

It's not that you have to sit down and logically come up with the best version of your ideal day. Just start now, do it, and as you get more ideas, feel free to add them. It's really lots of fun!

Do you know what the most successful athletes do?

Before the game or the event, they visualize the process and the successful outcome. Next, they focus on their feelings and live the success in their imagination.

They also do it after the game. Yes, whether the results were positive or negative, in their mind, they re-play it as positive (if the game went well) to further anchor those feelings. If the game was not successful, they create their own re-play where the result is successful.

So, no matter what happens, in their mind, they're always successful, and they enhance positive memories with visualizations.

Take a piece of paper and a pen, and set up a timer to make sure you entirely focus on this task and get in a flow. Make sure you avoid distractions, switch off your phone, etc.

I suggest you don't use your computer or phone—just a pen and paper.

Now, take a few deep breaths and allow yourself to think big. Perhaps you want to go full time with your passion; well, imagine yourself doing that for a living. Maybe you want to create an image of your camera and an amazing YouTube audience. You read comments from your tribe and feel happy. As you create that image, something else may appear in your mind.

You check up sales from your online courses and feel abundance. Or, someone calls you offering a speaking gig or wants to hire you as a coach. You attract new business opportunities and meet new business partners.

Then, another image may come to your mind…you wake up in a nice hotel, a new location. You hear seagulls; you love traveling and speaking, getting paid to talk about what you're passionate about.

One of my images is writing while overlooking the sea. Receiving emails from happy readers and being happy with their transformations.

I can smell the sea; the sound of the waves is calming. You'll have details coming up; some may seem unrealistic, but don't think too much about the *how*; just focus on the *why*.

Feel worthy and deserving; write everything down.

-When do you wake up, what does your bedroom look like?

-Where do you live? City? Nature? Penthouse, villa, a cozy apartment?

- Do you have children or a spouse?

-Do you have any pets?

-What's your morning routine? What do you love doing?

-Maybe you have a personal trainer and nutritionist?

-Do you wake up in a clean, organized space? Do you hire someone who cleans your house?

-What about your office? Where do you work? How do you communicate with your team?

-When and where do you eat your lunch? What do you do in the afternoon?

-What passions can you pursue in your free time?

-What does it feel like?

While doing it every day, you'll eventually create an image that will form into a step-by-step daily routine on your dream lifestyle design.

What I also love about this exercise is that you can see the future you, so it's essentially a stronger version of the current you. The new you, has better habits and mindsets. What you can start doing is to adapt your future habits right now. This is how you'll bridge the new you with the current you and eventually launch the new version of you, when what you see as a dream vision now, will be your reality.

Your subconscious mind will get comfortable with it and will lead you to take inspired action like an invisible force.

Whenever you feel down, close your eyes and focus on people who make you feel good and appreciate you. In business, it can be people like your regular clients, or business partners you admire. Create an image of that feeling and re-use it whenever you need it. Most people focus on the negative and on what they don't want. Ever since I started to focus on that simple trick while at the same time writing, "I attract amazing people to my biz and life" in my journal, I permitted myself to leave negative environments and made new positive friendships. It's essential you do these exercises, even for a few minutes every day. Most subconscious mind experts recommend doing them after waking up or before you go to bed.

Shift Yourself Out of Overwhelm (works like magic!)

As long as you focus on what you can control and give it your full attention and stay consistent, you'll manifest success. So how to make it happen? And what to do when something negative happens or when we feel overwhelmed or stuck?

Here's my best tip:

If you're feeling overwhelmed, you need to ask yourself why and why you think it's terrible to feel overwhelmed. You see, if you go to the gym and want to get results that last, there will be periods of time when your muscles will need to adjust, and so they'll feel overwhelmed.

Same with business and life. When you're committed to growth, there will be situations that will make you feel overwhelmed; why try to escape from that? What you can control is your perception and how you react to what you think is a feeling of overwhelm.

First of all, ask yourself how someone you really look up to, someone who you consider successful in your field, would react to a situation that makes you feel overwhelmed. What would he or she do? Also, do you think that this person also felt overwhelmed at some stage? Instead of feeling reactive, they found some proactive way to move forward.

For example, if you're feeling overwhelmed with your workload, you can look for people and resources to help you accomplish your goals faster. Great leaders don't lead alone, and they're not afraid to ask for help.

Exercise:
-What makes you feel stressed, and how can you turn that around into excitement?

-What's the number 1 thing you need to be doing daily to get closer to your goals?

-What makes you feel overwhelmed? Why are you feeling that way? Is it because you are doing too much or too little?

-What would be a small daily win to make you easily go to sleep with satisfaction? Why not start today and enjoy every little win on your journey?

Be a LOA-Preneur, You Can Do This!

You now have everything you need to overcome your limiting mindsets and shift into the new, more empowered version of yourself!

Keep growing and keep expanding. The world needs you and your work!

You're in the process of manifesting an incredible impact and abundance, not only in your business but in all areas of your life.

I sincerely believe in YOU!

Thank you for reading with an open mind and open heart! If you enjoyed this book, I'd really appreciate your honest review on Amazon.

Let others know the number one thing you learned from this book and who you think should read it! Also, what makes this book different from similar books you've read in the past?

The next page contains practical resources from various business experts to help you on your journey!

Expert Resources and Biz Ideas for LOA Entrepreneurs

Disclaimer – These are NOT paid endorsements. I don't receive any compensation from recommending any these experts, their work, or any of the websites mentioned.

Personally, I learned a lot from all of them, and I hope you'll also gain value from their teachings! However, before getting invested into anything, always be sure to do your own research.

Gundi Gabrielle's books: Gundi is an expert in book publishing, so if you'd like to write and publish your own books, I urge you to check out her work: www.sassyzengirl.com

You may also discover other business ideas, her work will help you if you want to be an online entrepreneur or influencer, and you desire a freedom-based, lifestyle business (so that you can work from home or while traveling the world on your own terms).

George Kao's books, videos, and articles– George is an authentic marketing expert who helped me a lot in my business and life. If you feel like the mainstream marketing tactics are too pushy or salesy for your brand, I encourage you to follow George's work. He's very generous with his free content on YouTube.
www.georgekao.com

Michele PW: Michele is an amazing author, both in fiction and non-fiction. I especially recommend her love-based copywriting books, if you'd like to craft a message that really resonates with your audience without using any fear or manipulation-based tactics. Love-based strategies work very well long term if you want to build your brand and reputation: www.michelepw.com

Miles Beckler's videos and articles: Miles calls himself 'the most helpful online marketer in the world,' and he truly lives up to that expectation! It's not easy to find someone so passionate about helping others. If you feel like your business might benefit from learning more about digital marketing, I highly recommend Miles' blog and YouTube channel. Miles is very generous with his free content! If you want to build your brand on YouTube, grow your expert business, or perhaps you want to grow a blog, I highly recommend you follow his tutorials:
www.milesbeckler.com

Michal Essek's articles, books, and videos: If you're a creative or artist and would like to start selling your art, I highly recommend you check out Michael's blog for creative print-on-demand business ideas:
www.michaelessek.com

Law of Attr-Action for Entrepreneurs

Practical Business Ideas

1. Offer freelance services on websites such as Upwork, Fiverr, and Freelancer.com (or look for freelance websites online).

2. Create courses and upload to www.Udemy.com

3. Write books and publish on Amazon, using www.kdp.com

4. Make designs and upload to Amazon Merch, Redbubble, and other Print-On-Demand websites.

5. Create photography and vectors. Then upload them to different stock websites.

6. Open a motivational YouTube channel (or any channel based on your expertise) and offer coaching to your subscribers. You can also design online courses for self-study.

Wishing you the best of luck, peace, and prosperity!
Elena

Free LOA Newsletter + Bonus Gift

To help you AMPLIFY what you've learned in this book, I'd like to offer you a free, digital copy of my **LOA Workbook – a powerful, FREE 5-day program (eBook & audio)** designed to help you raise your vibration while eliminating resistance and negativity.

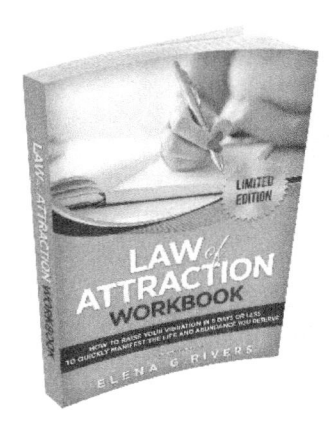

To sign up for free, visit the link below now:
www.loaforsuccess.com/newsletter

If you come across any technical problems, just email:

support@LOAforSuccess.com

More Books Written by Elena G.Rivers

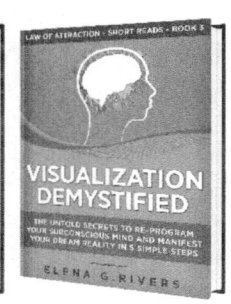

For more information visit: www.LOAforSuccess.com or search for Elena G.Rivers on Amazon!

Money Mindset Audiobook

Now available on Audible!

Thank You for your continued interest and support, we hope you'll find these publications helpful on your LOA journey!

Elena & LOA for Success

Printed in Great Britain
by Amazon